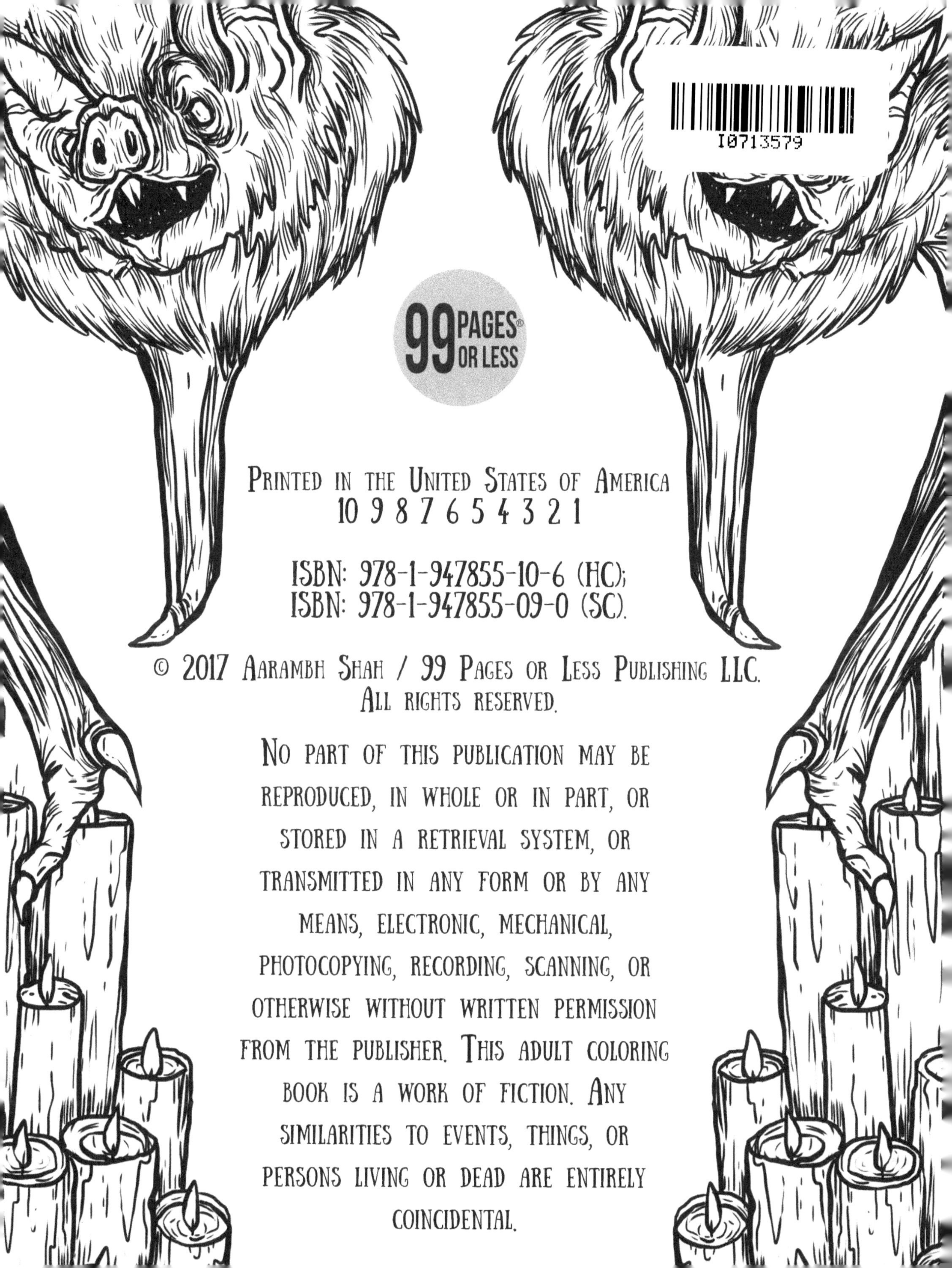

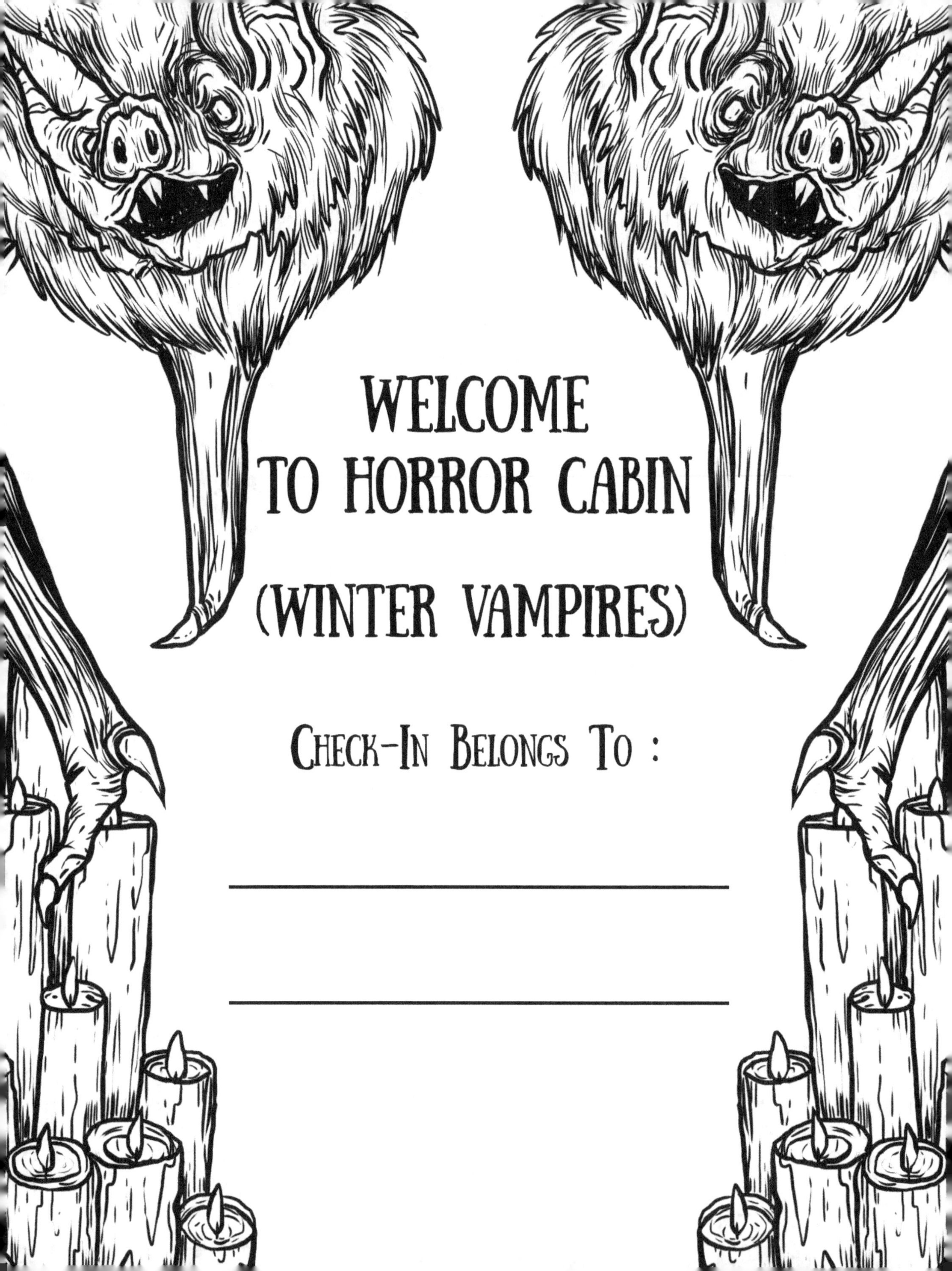

WELCOME
TO HORROR CABIN

(WINTER VAMPIRES)

CHECK-IN BELONGS TO :

____

____

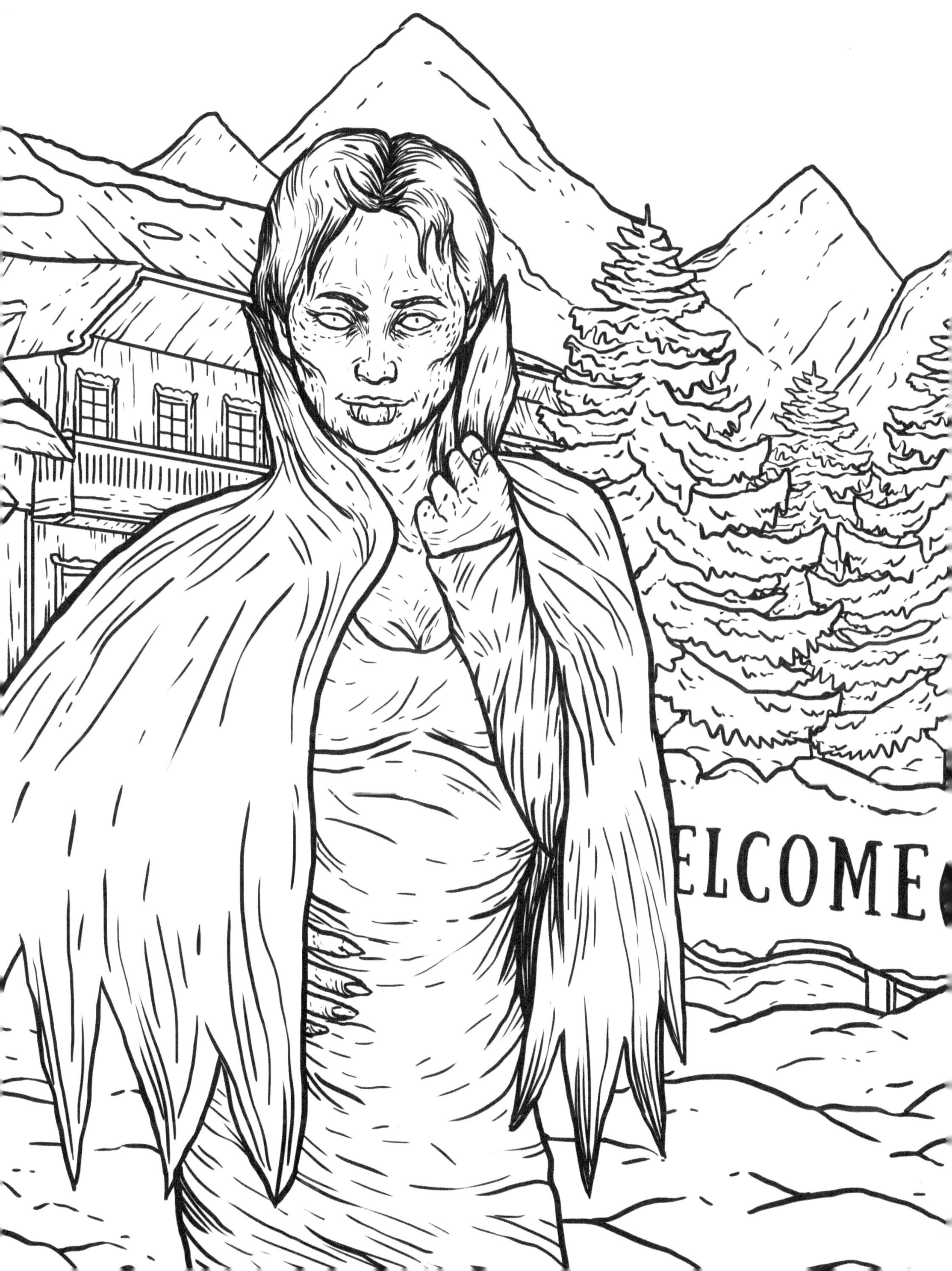
ELCOME

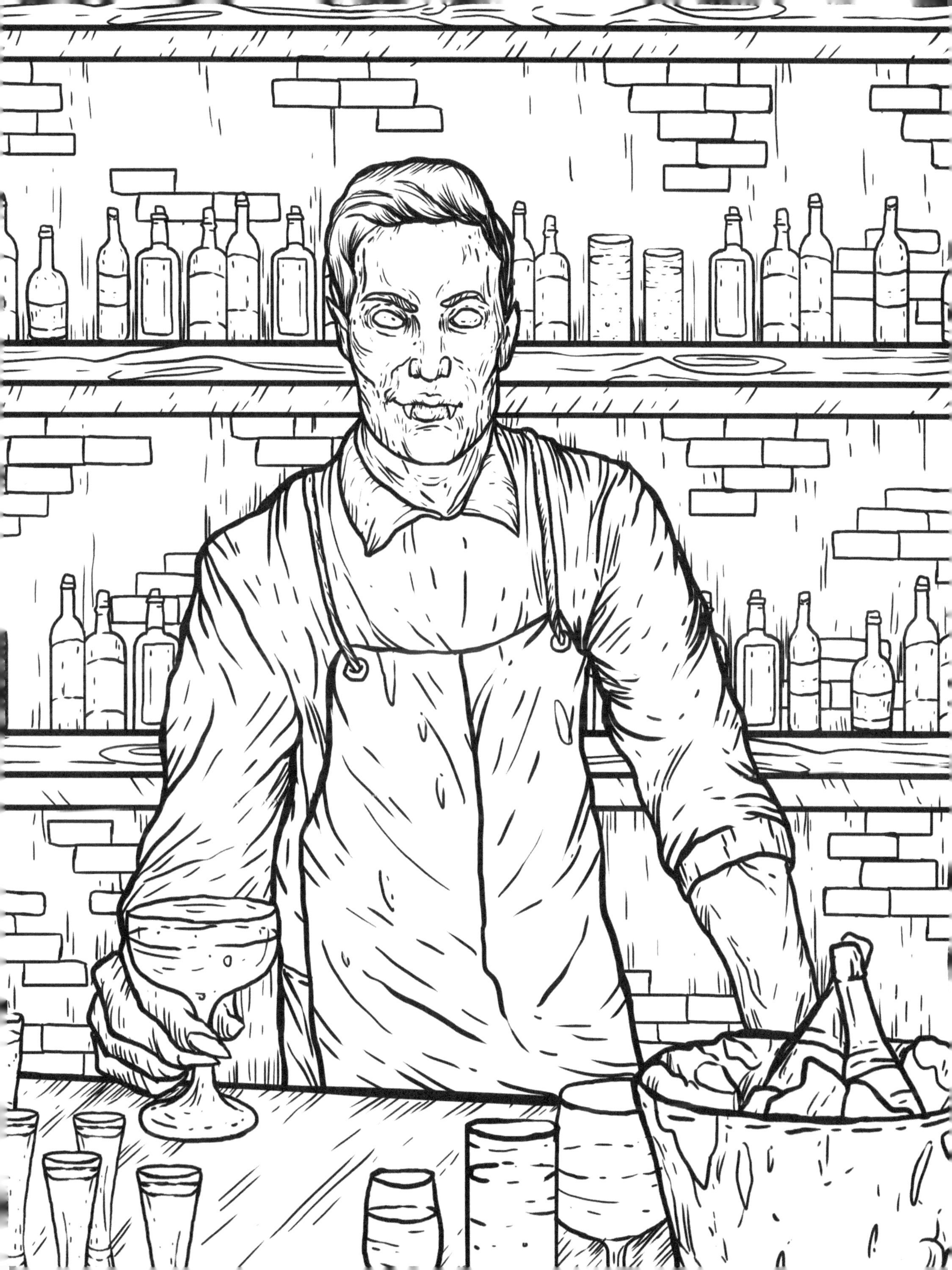

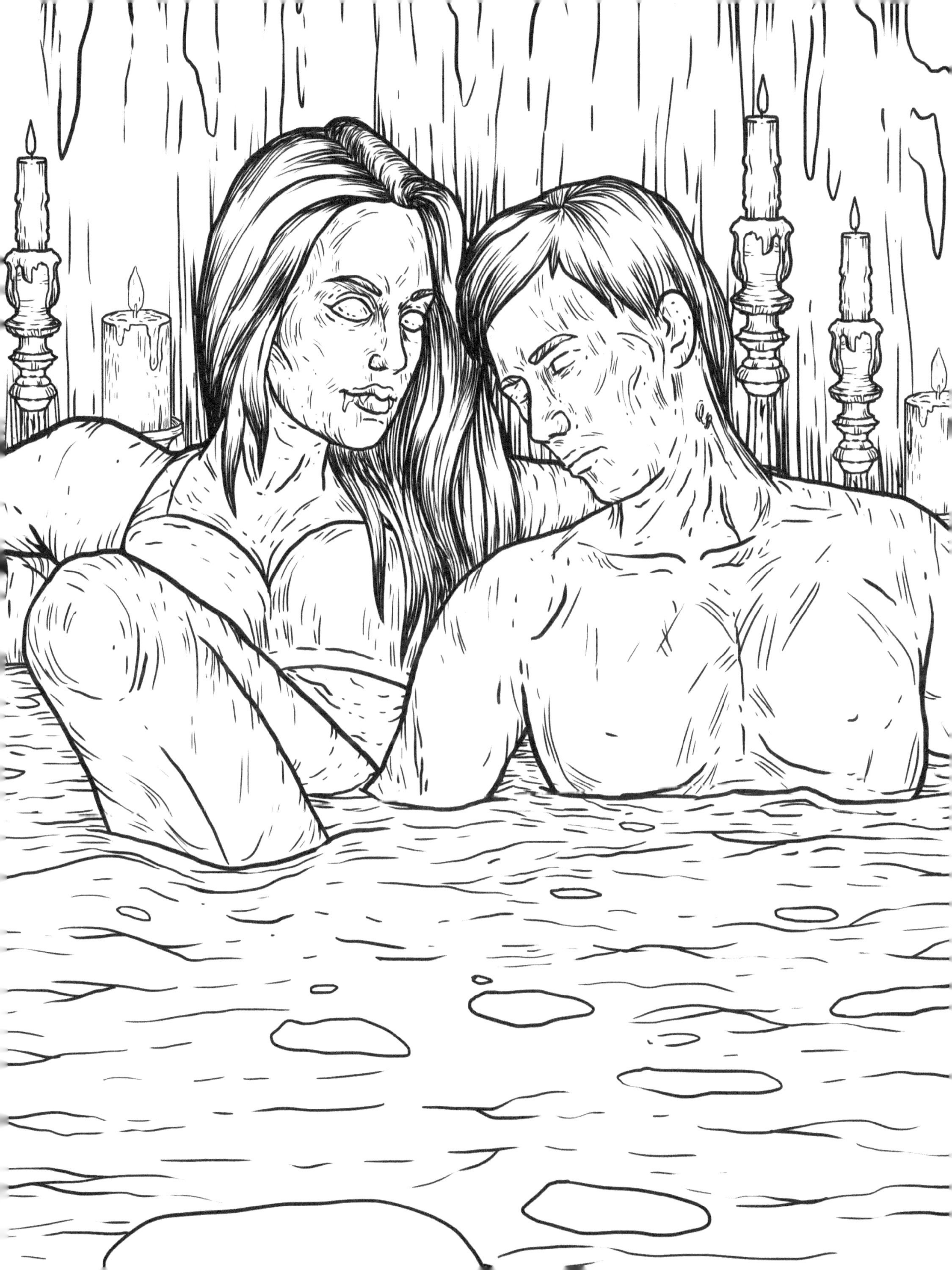

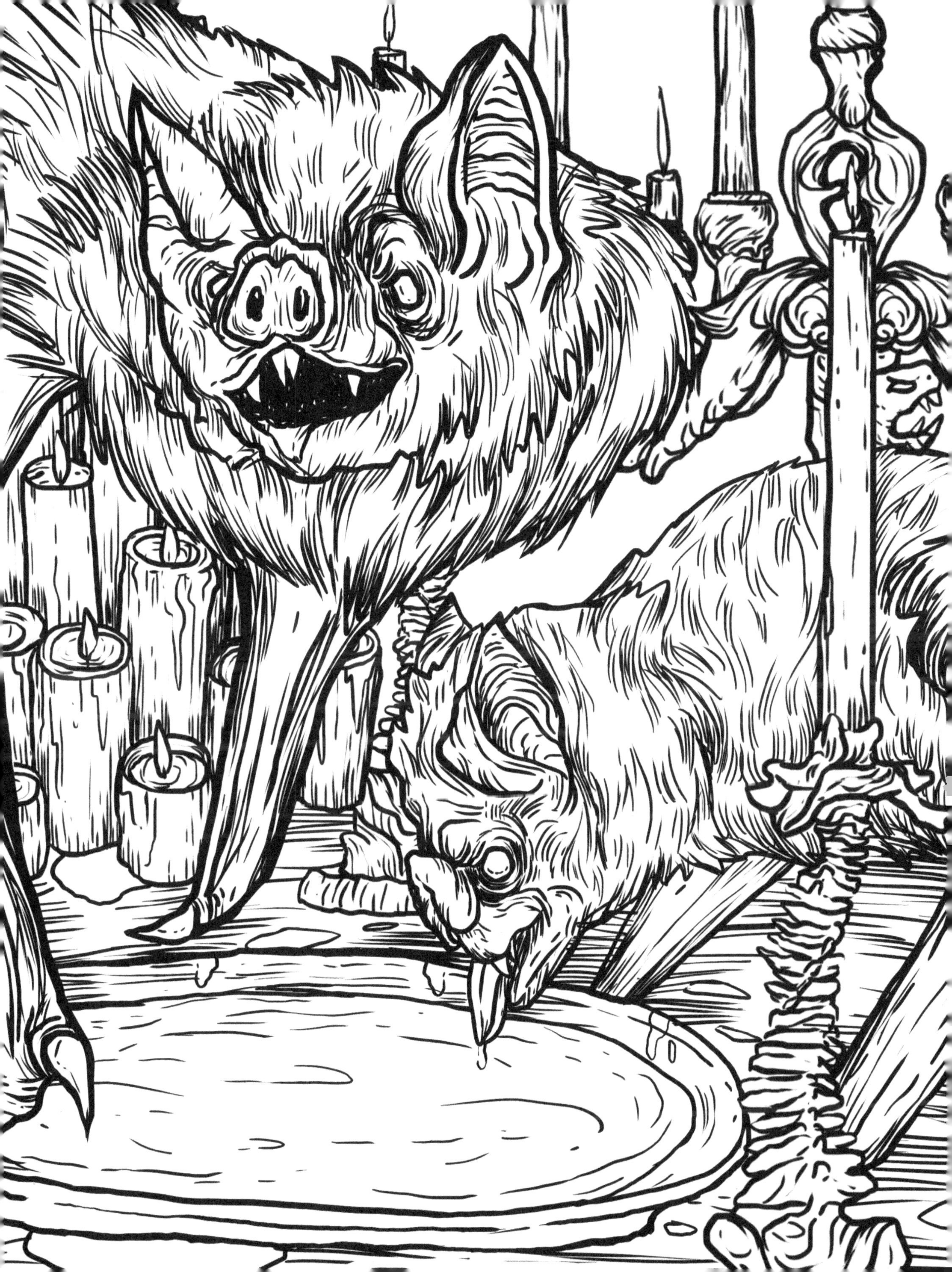

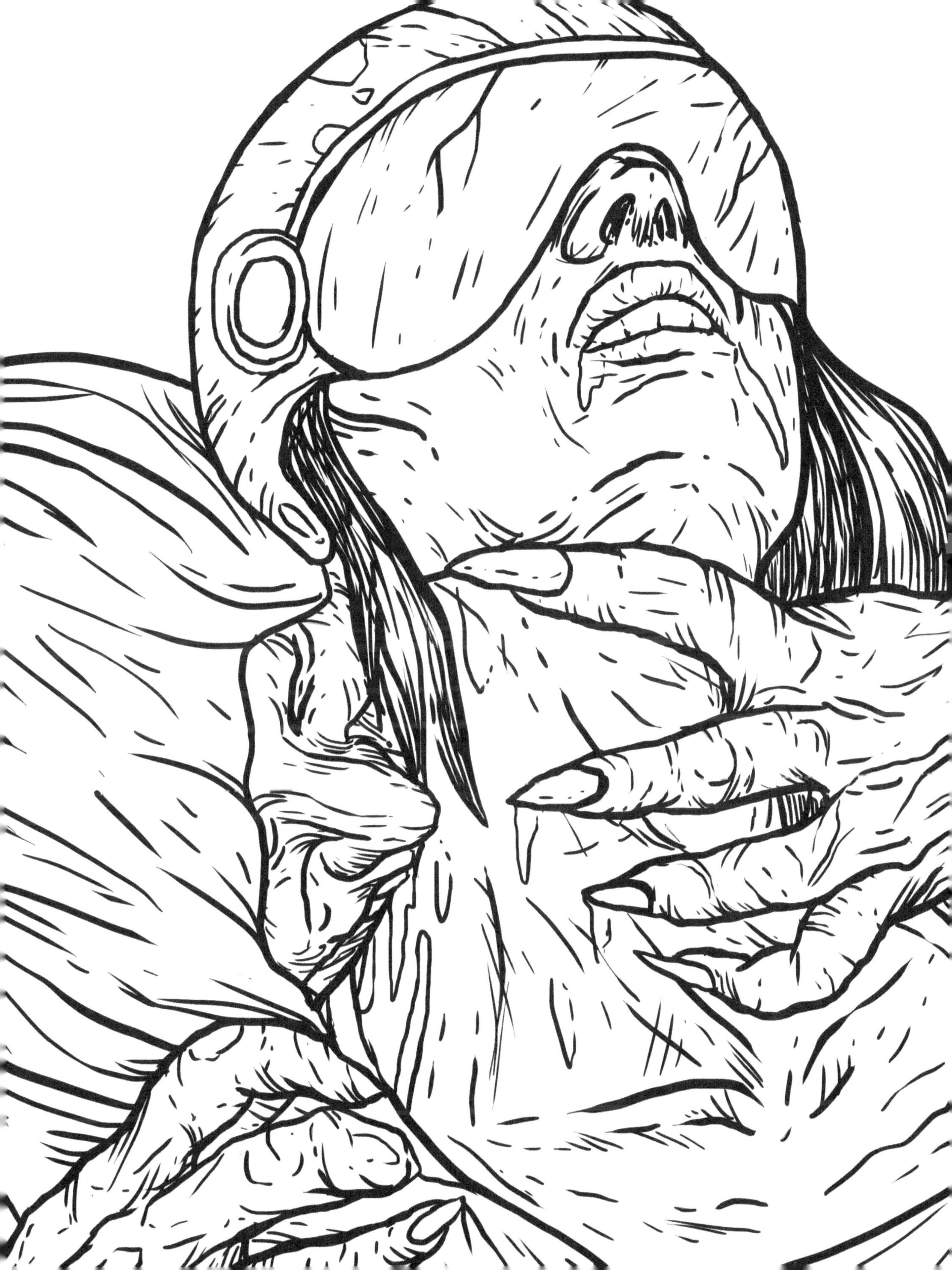

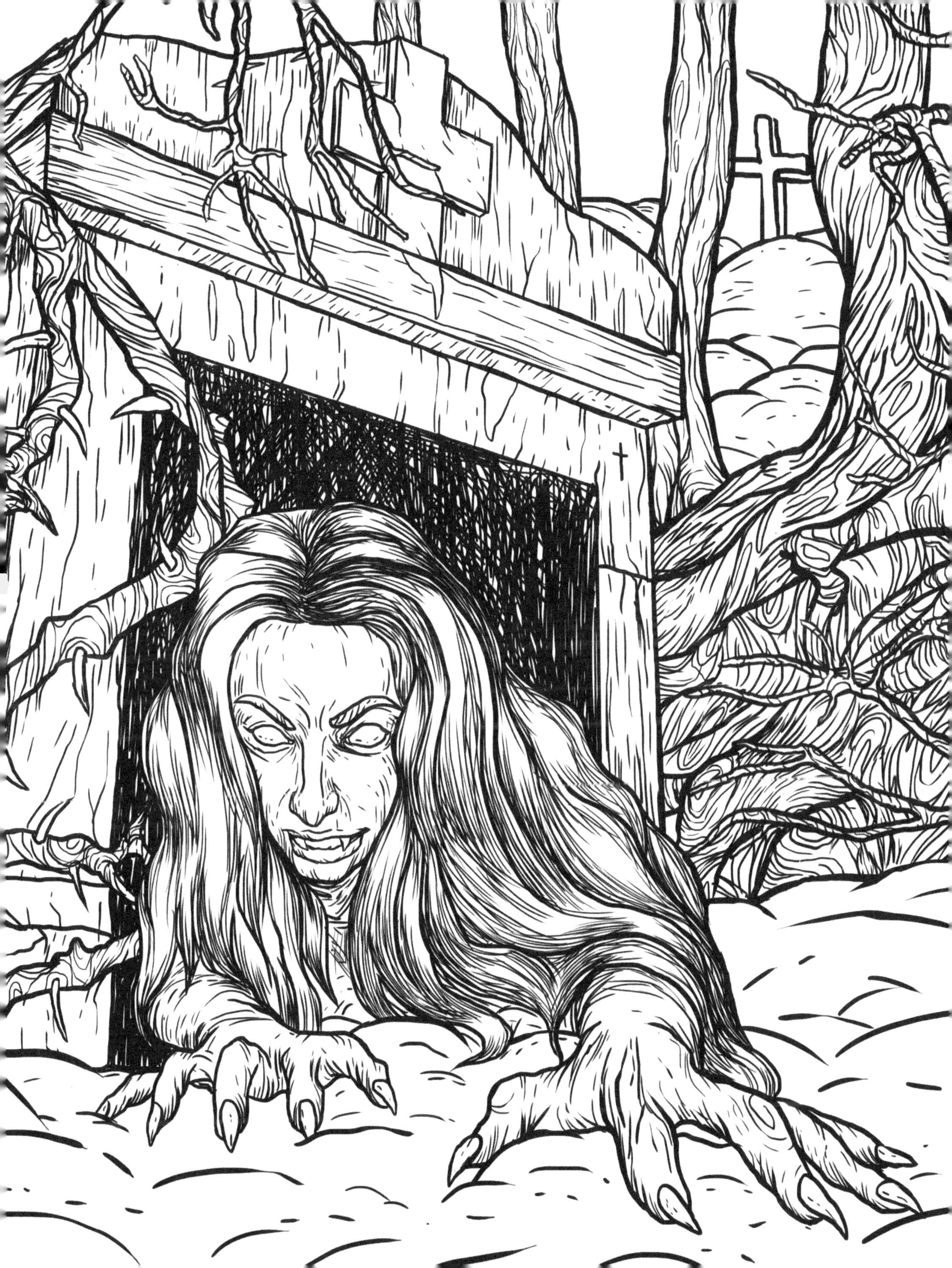

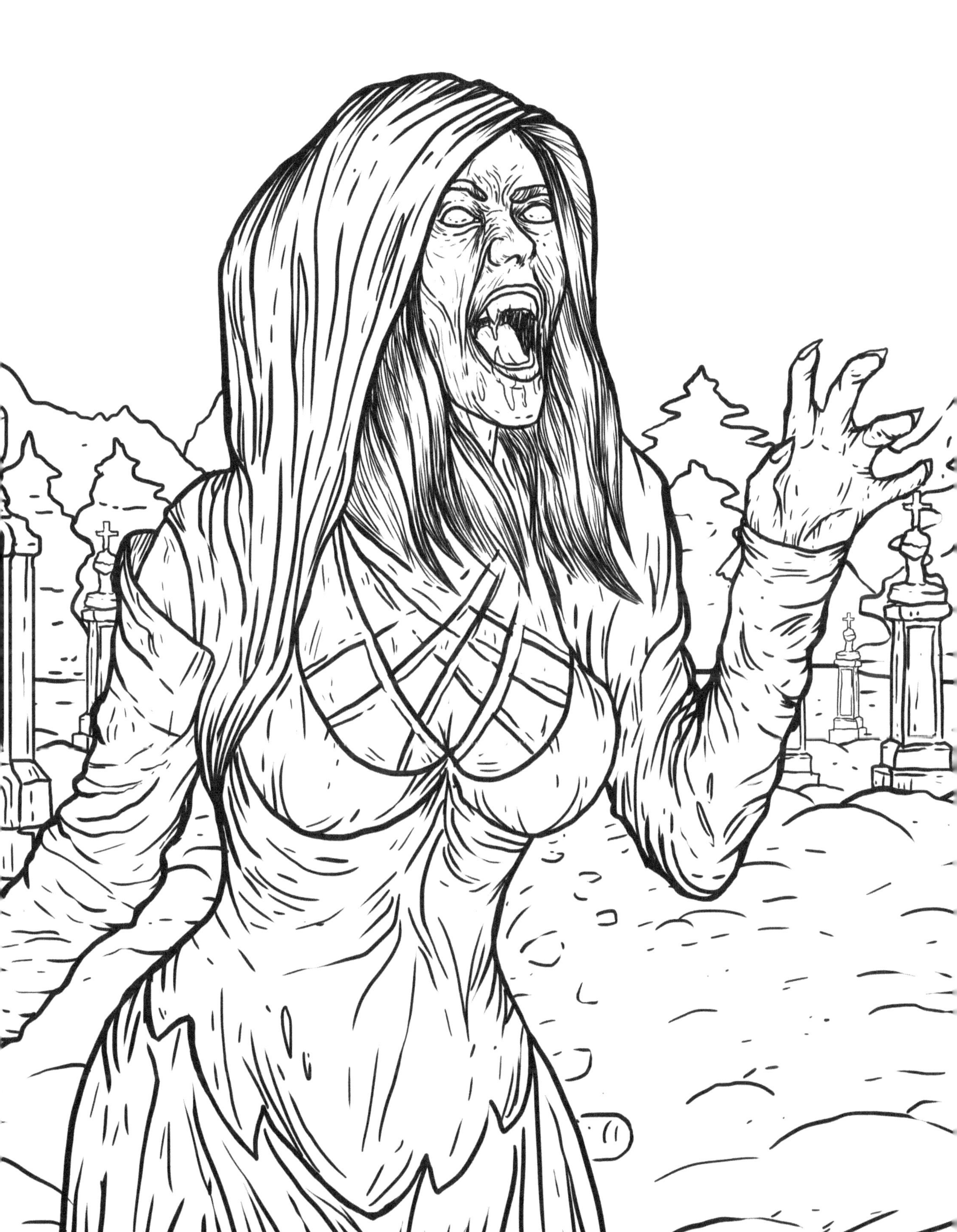

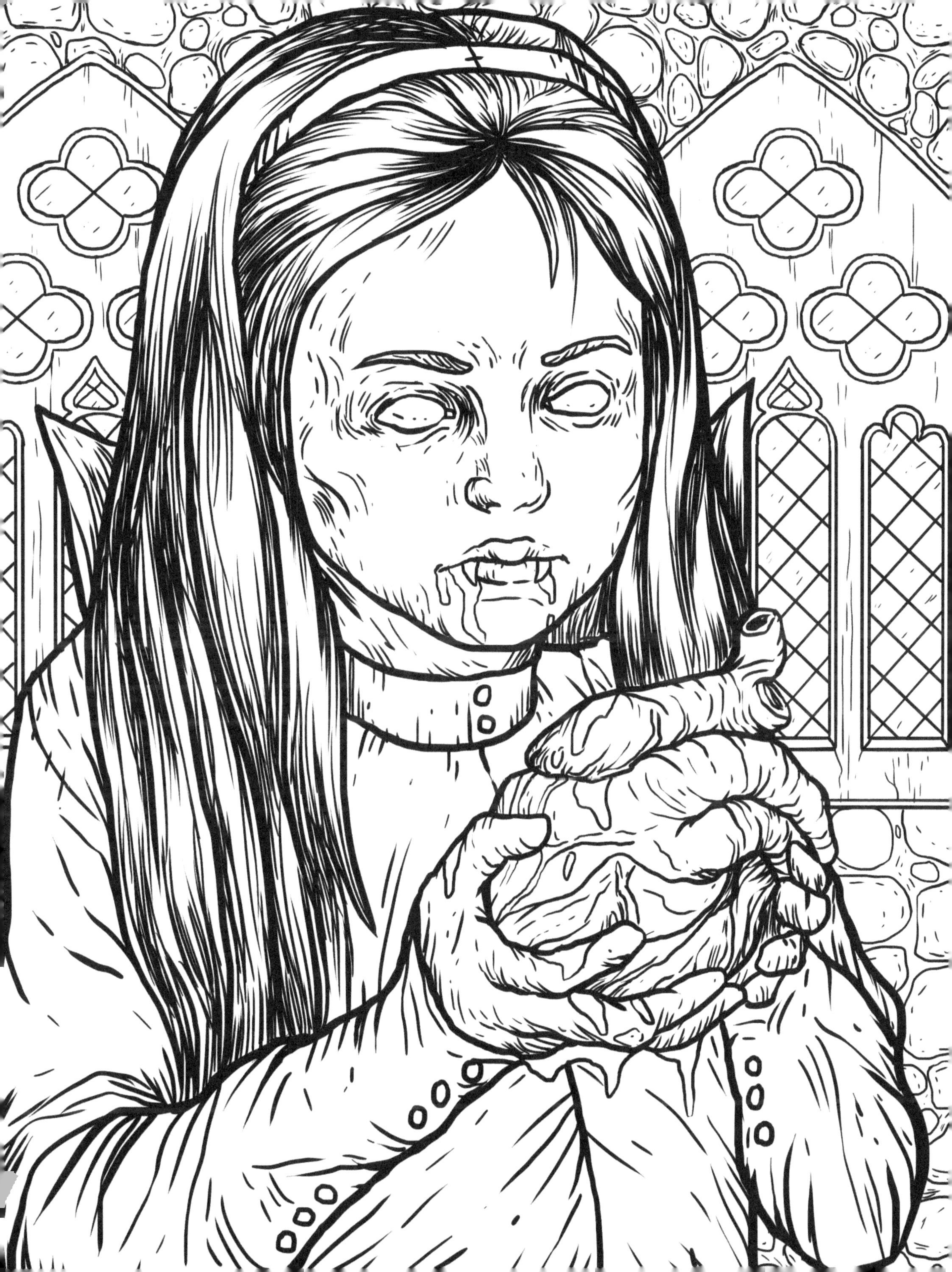

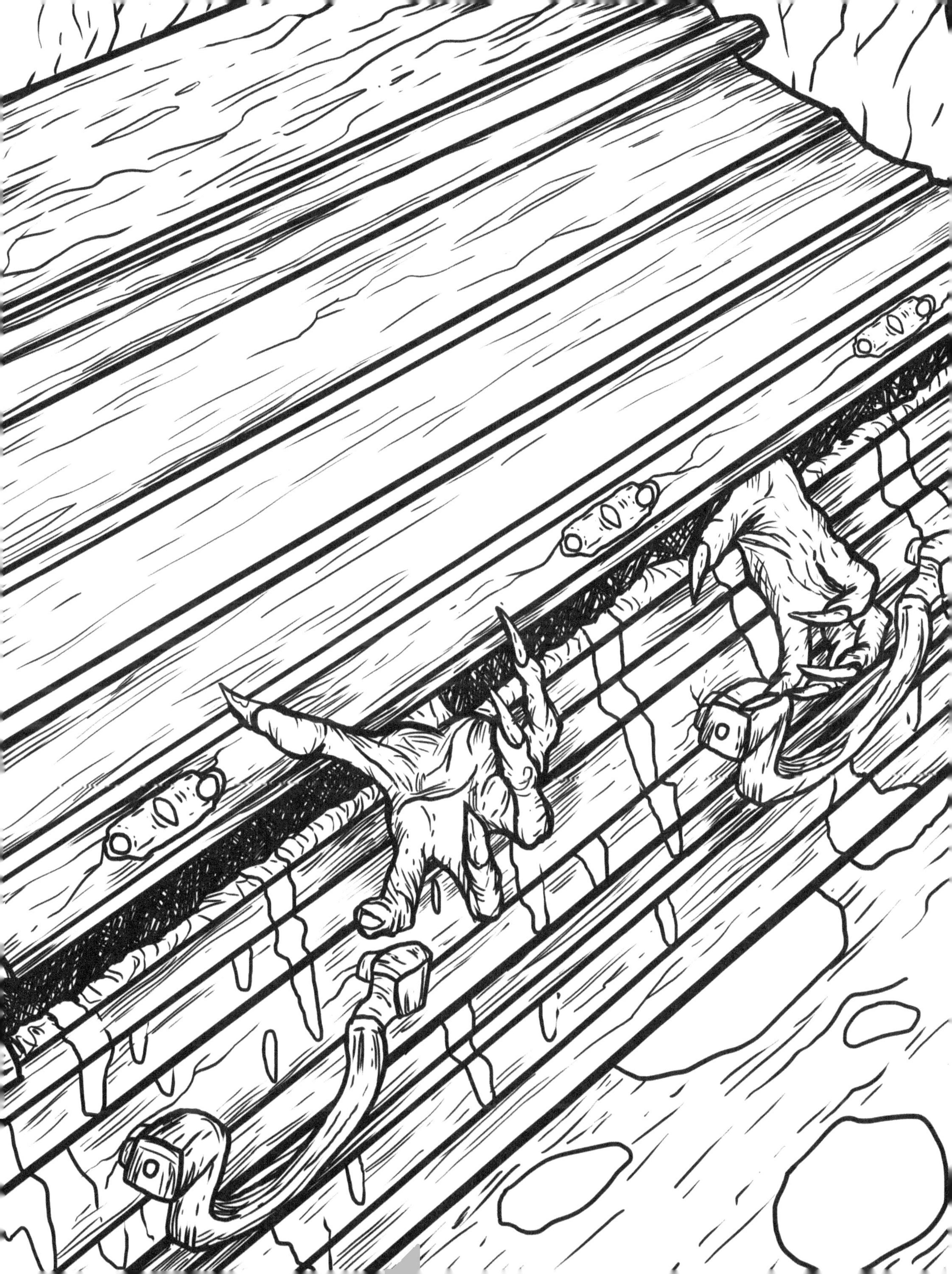

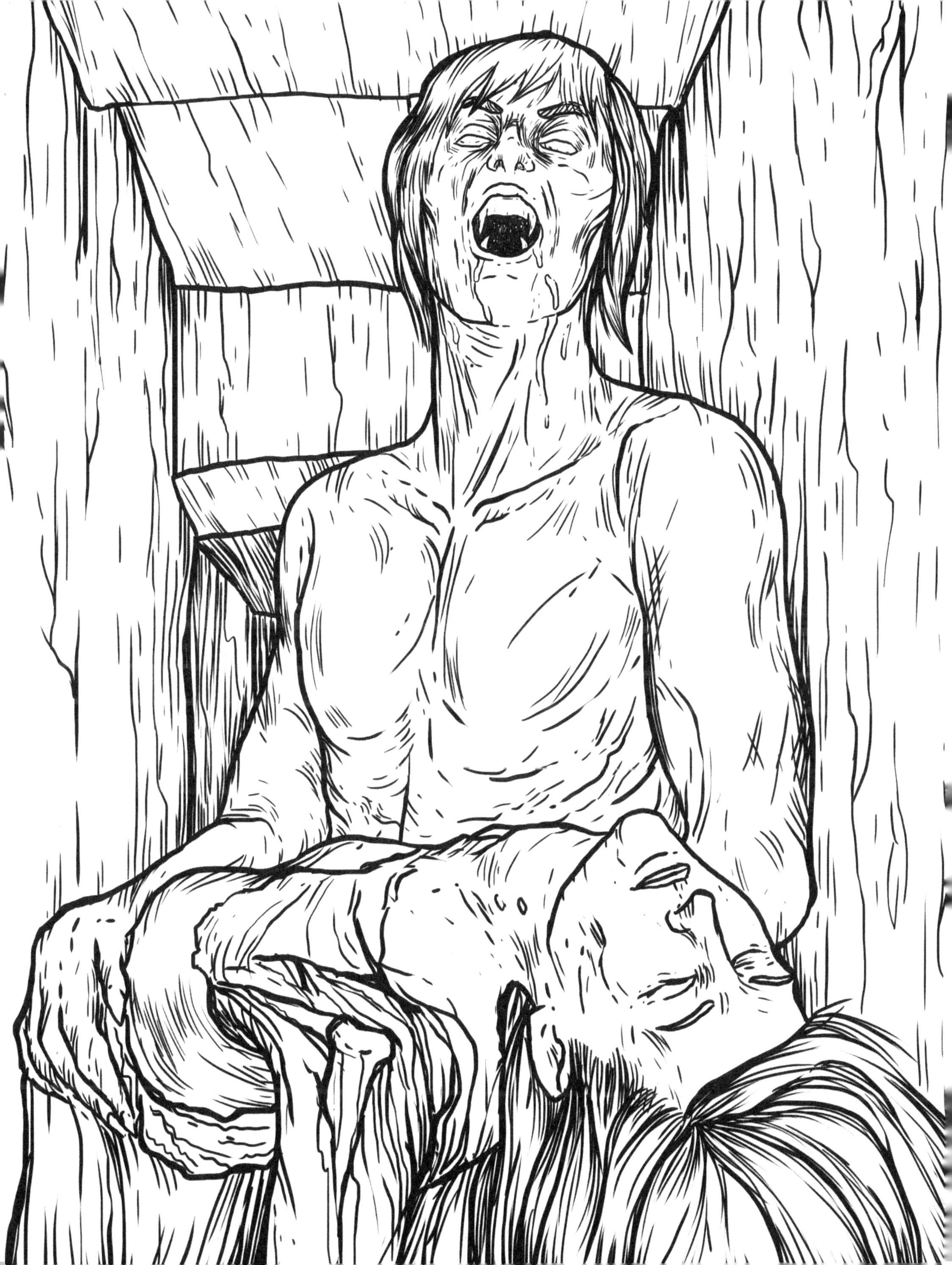

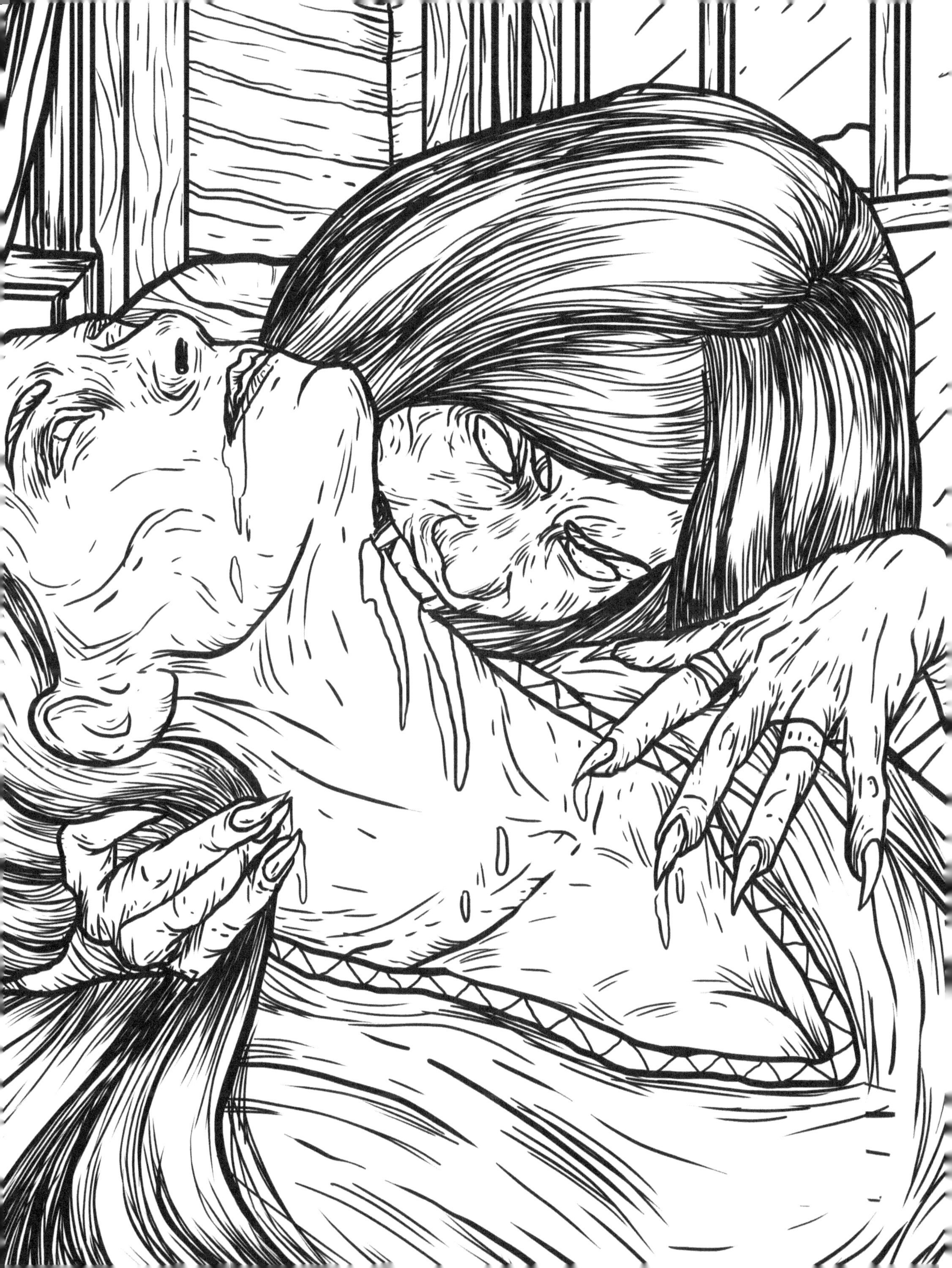

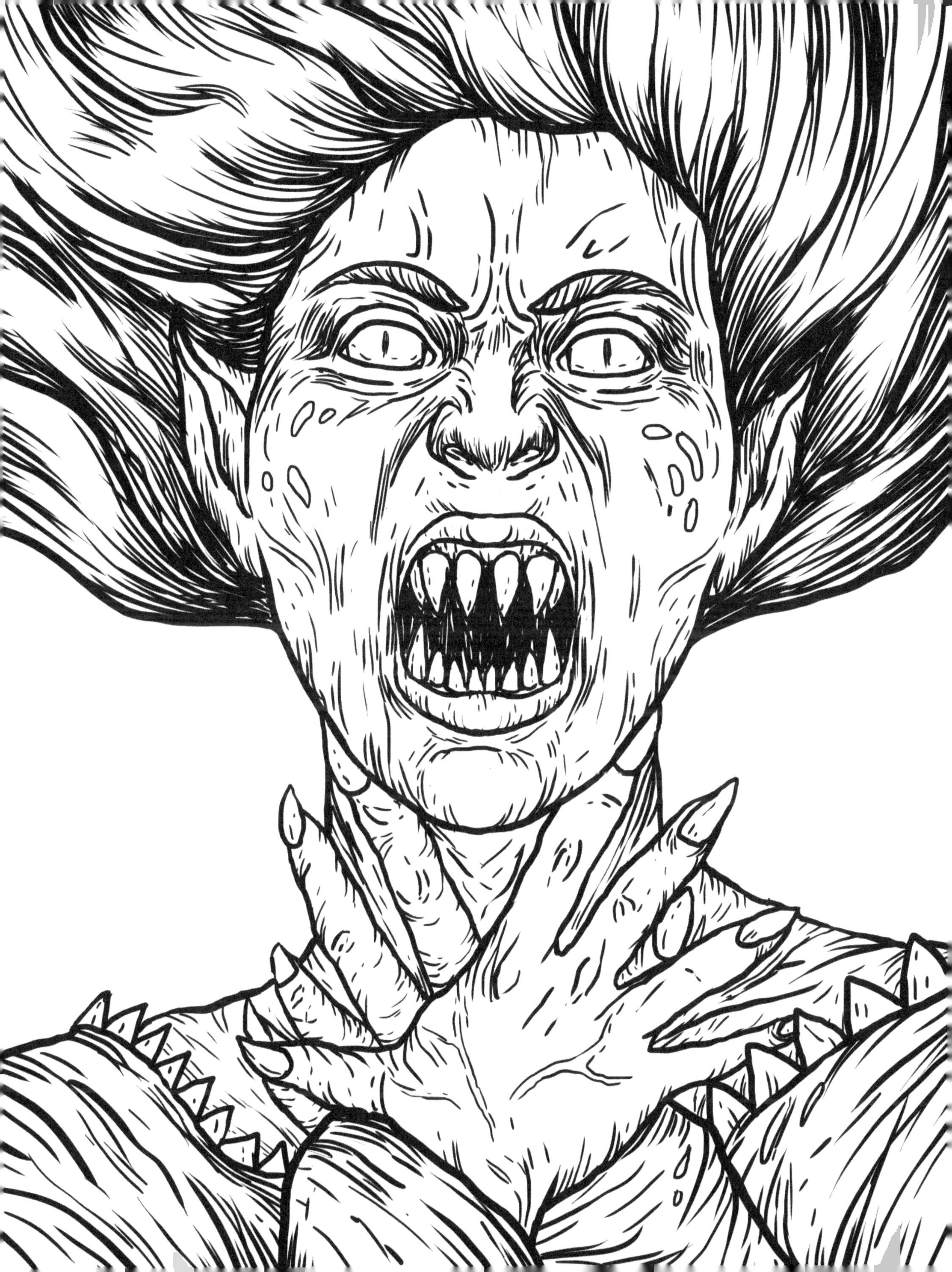

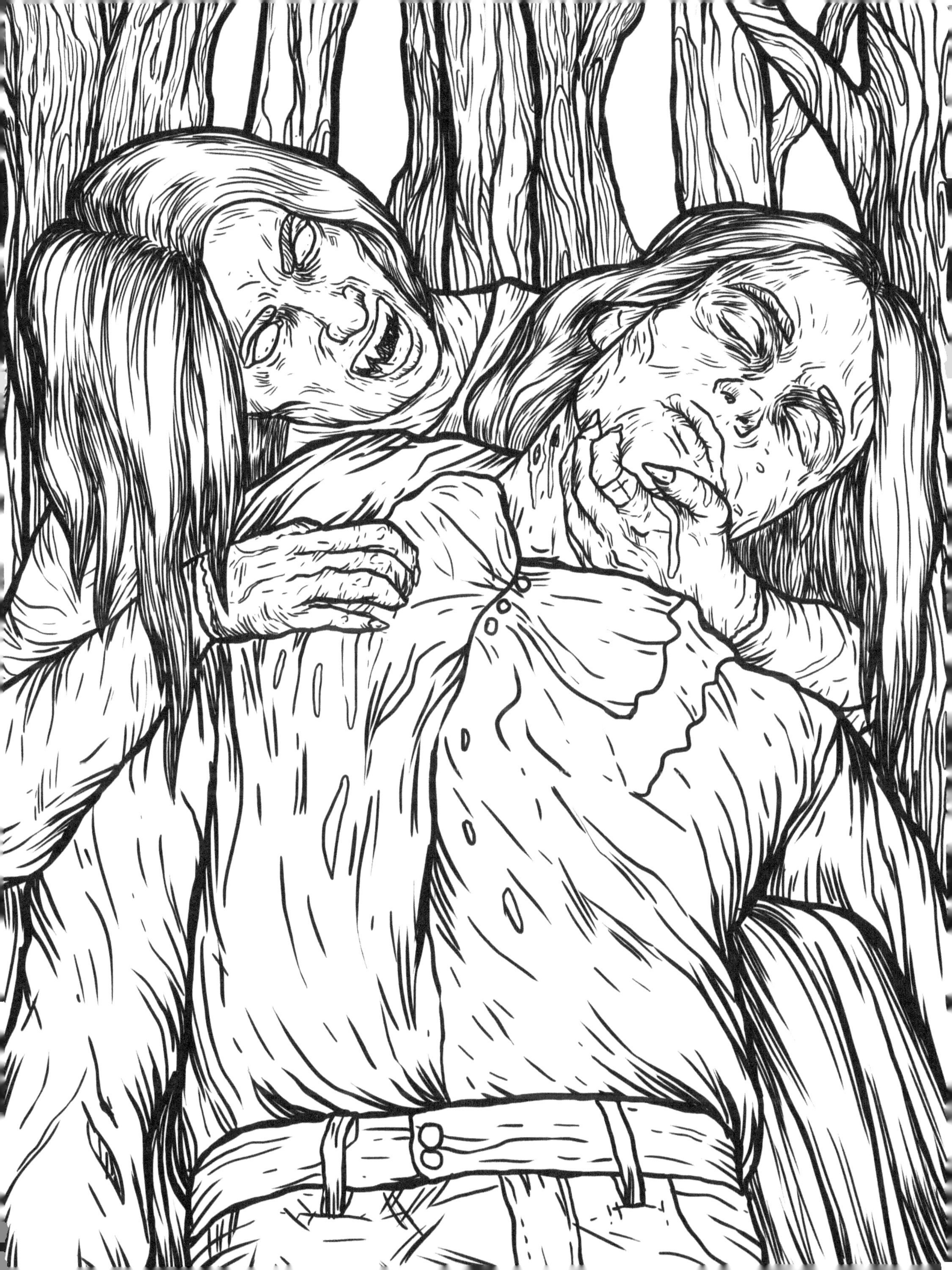

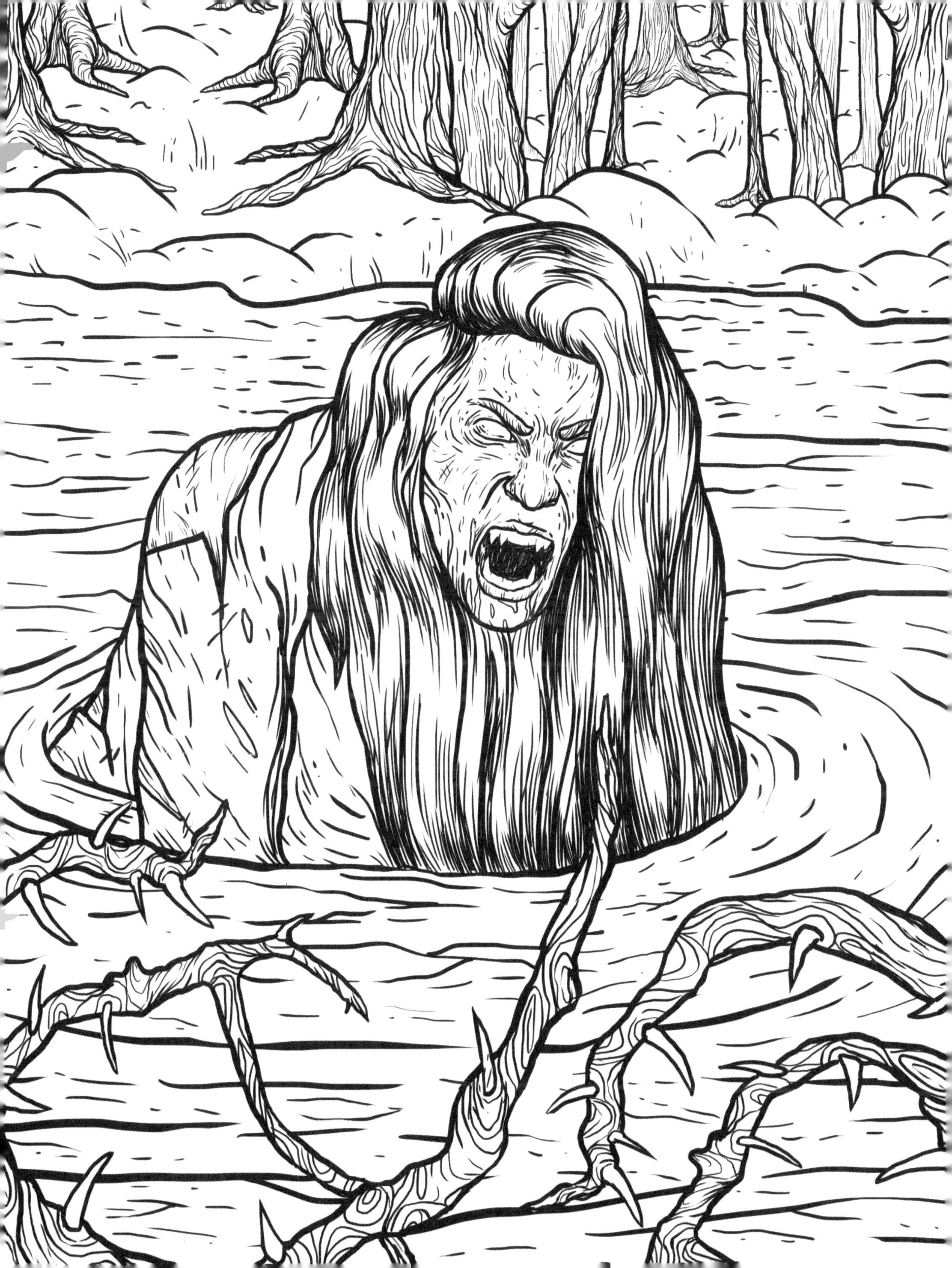

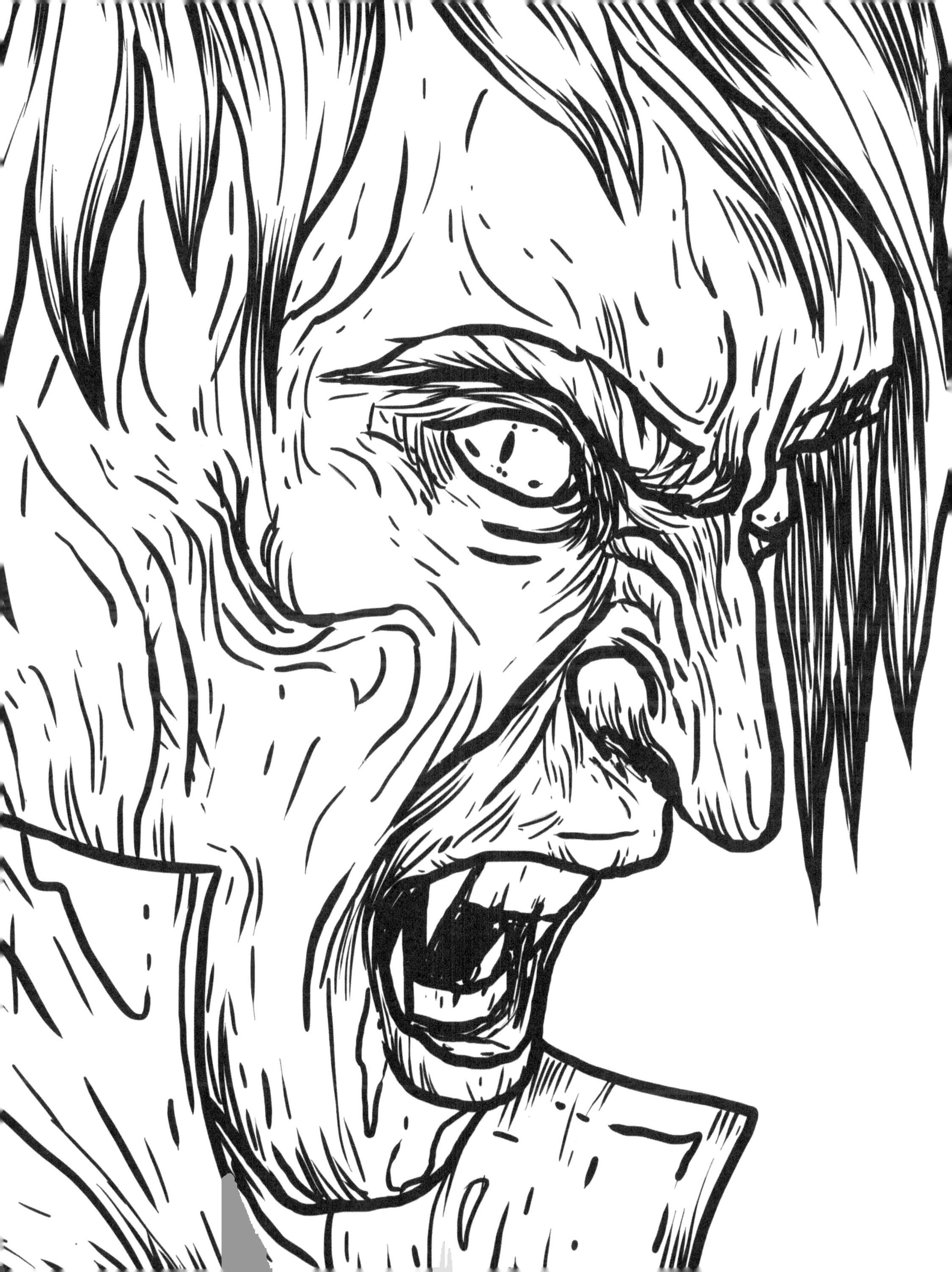

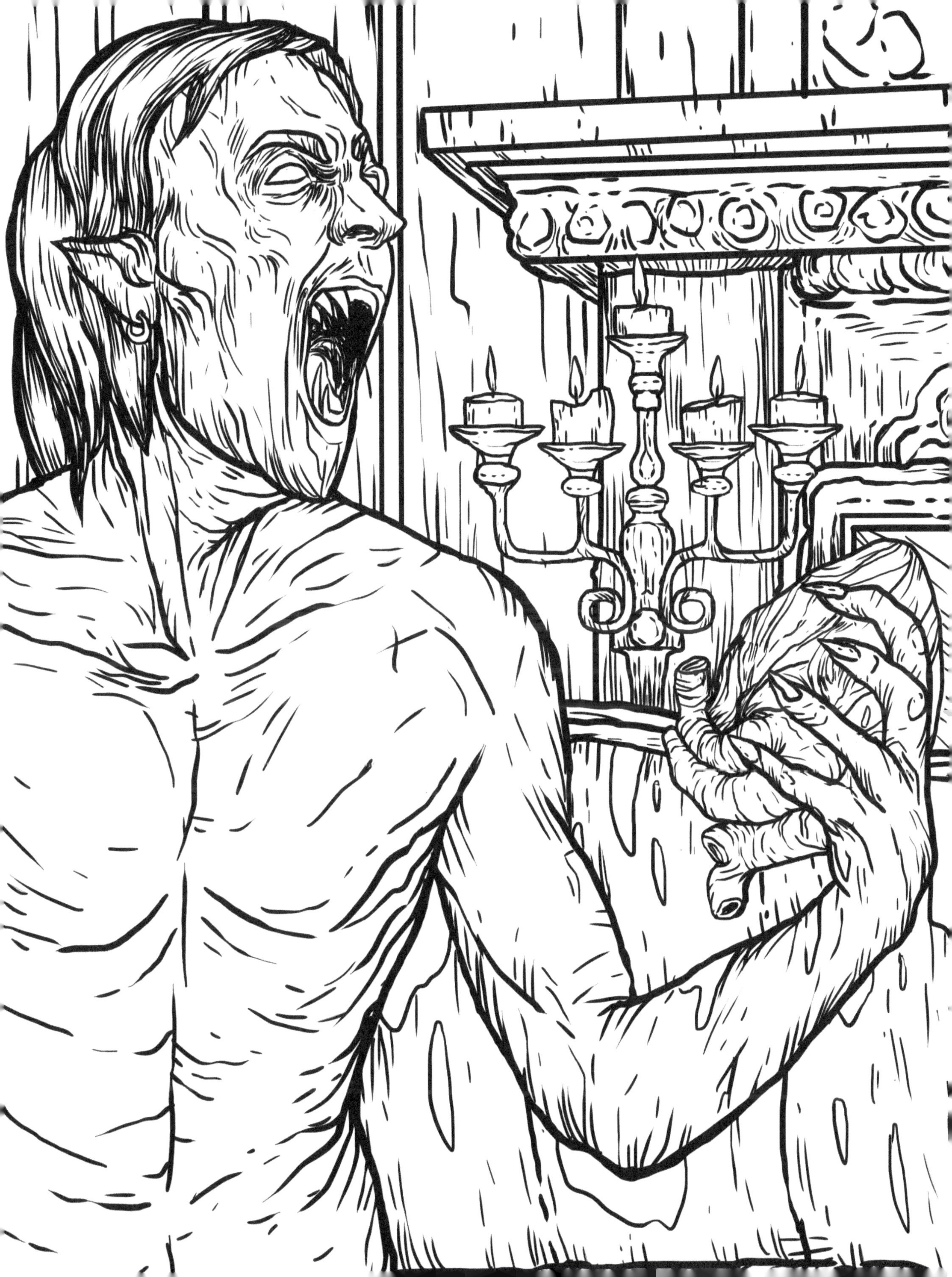

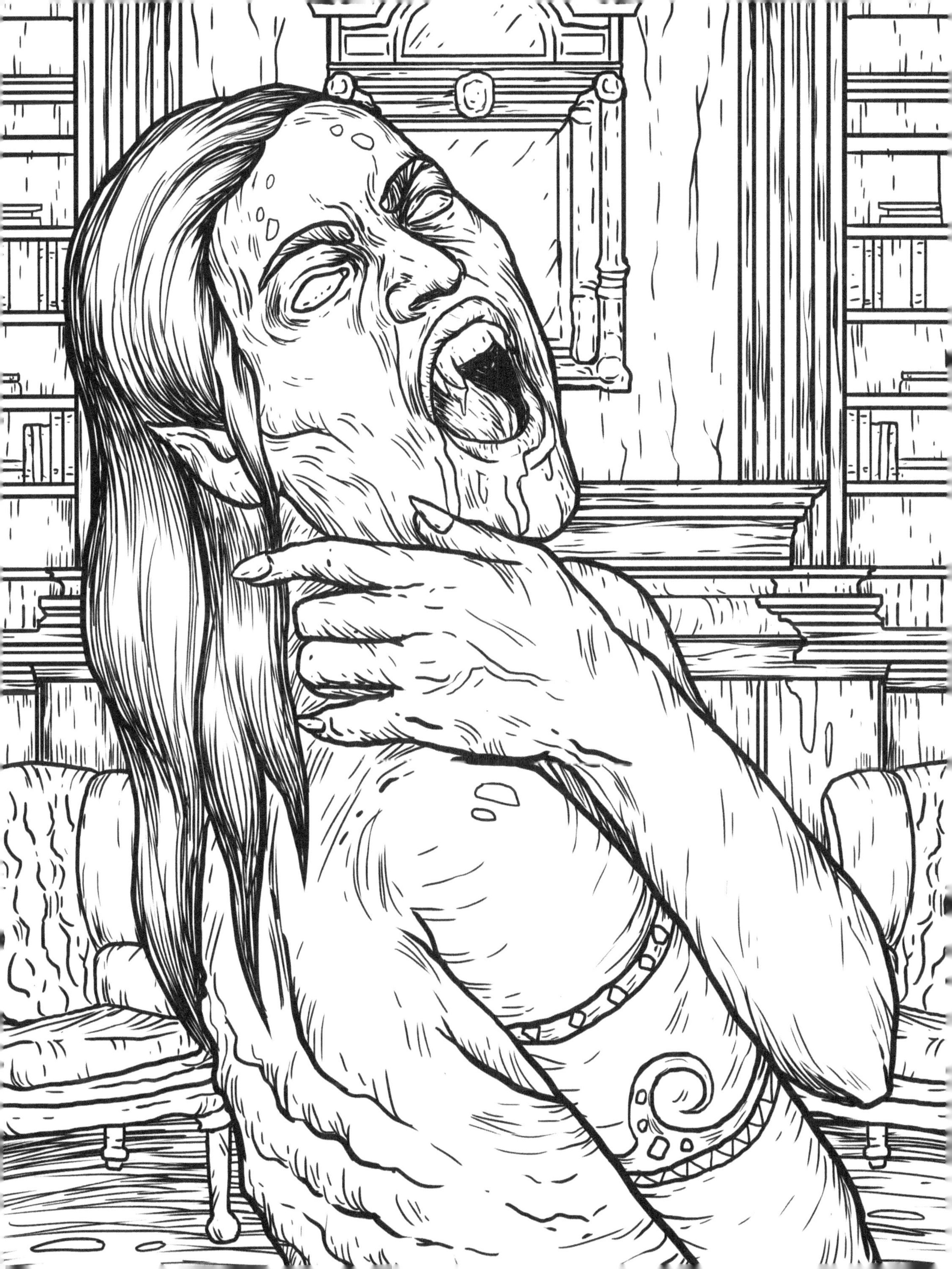

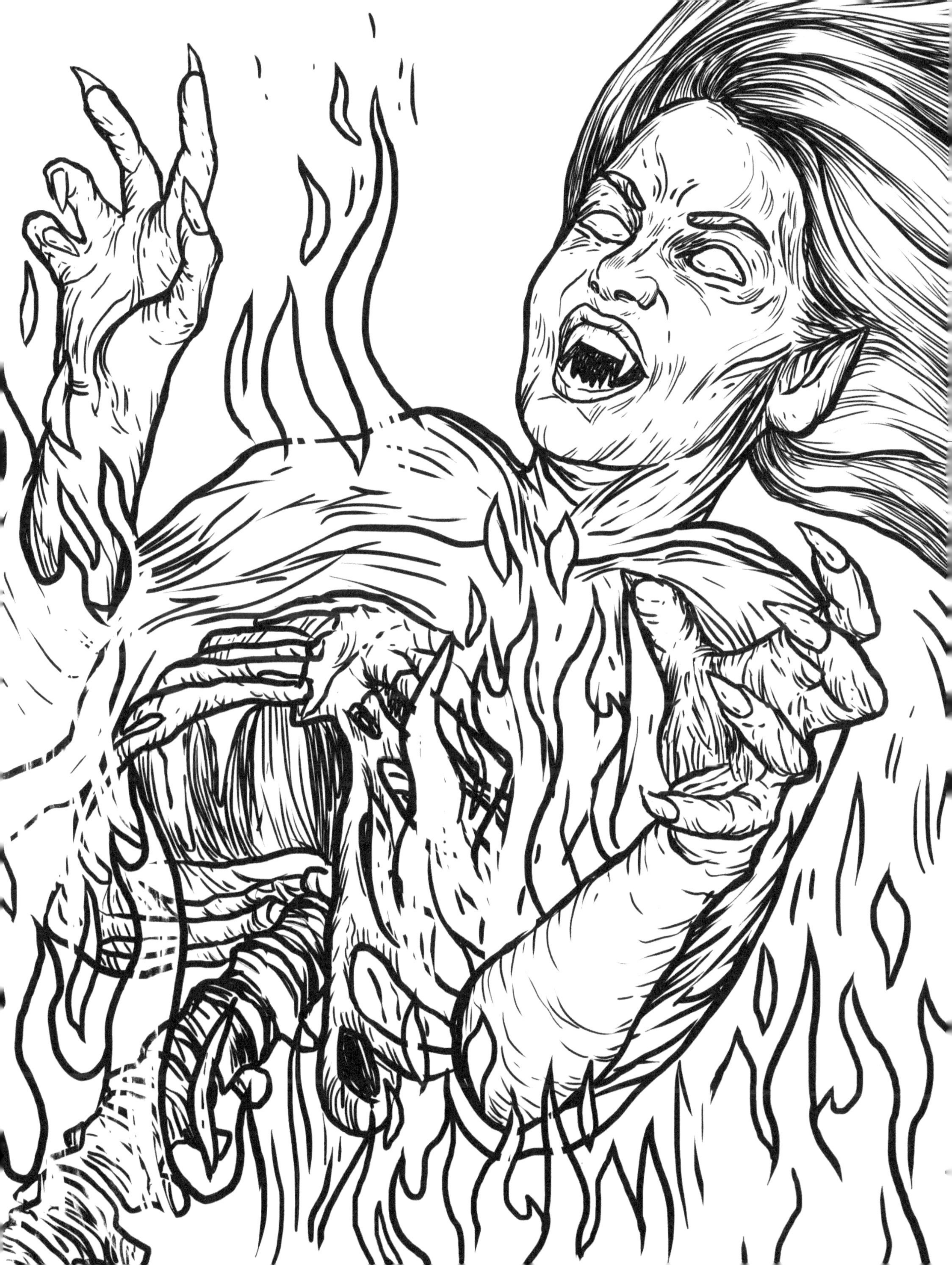

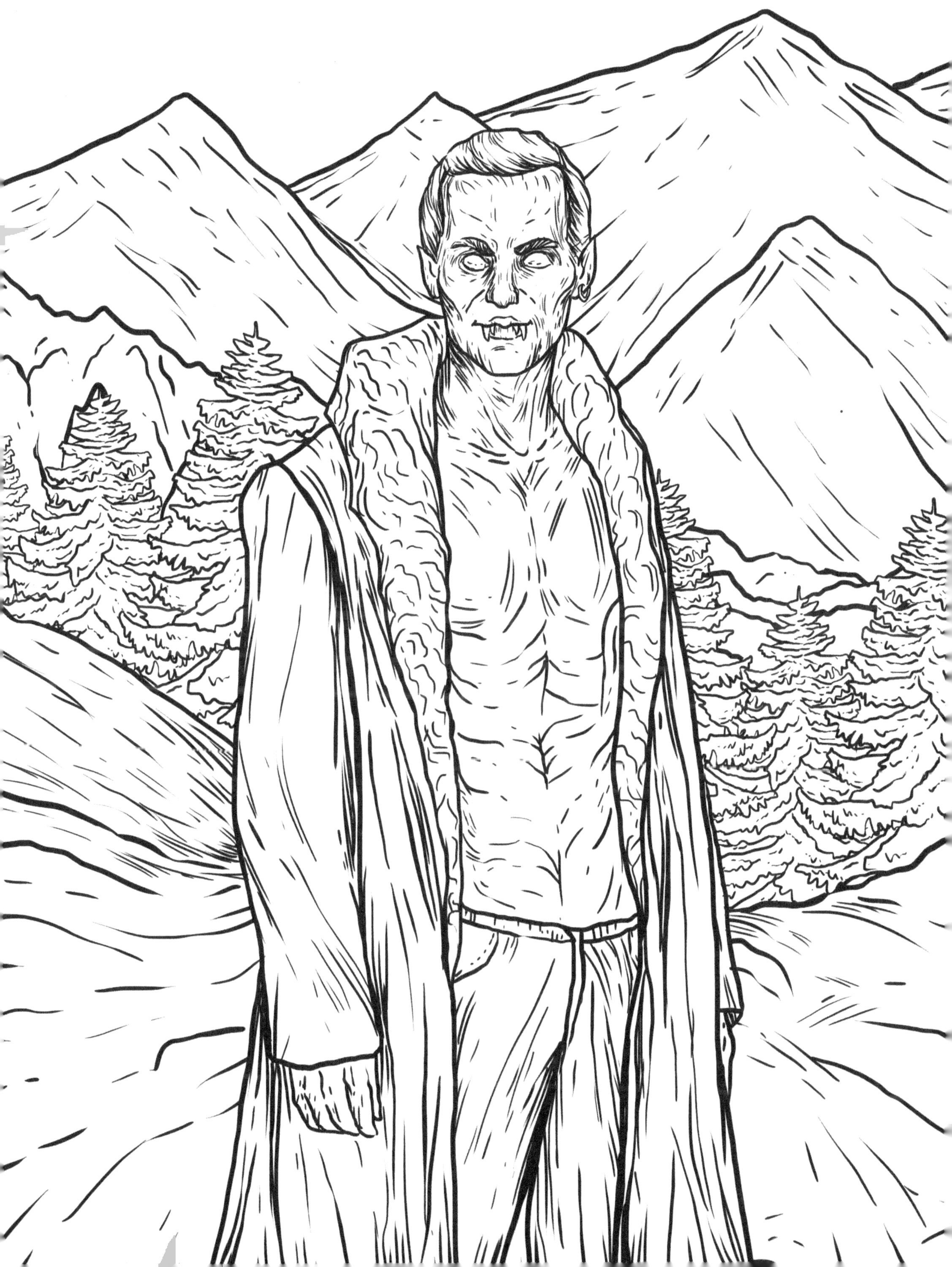

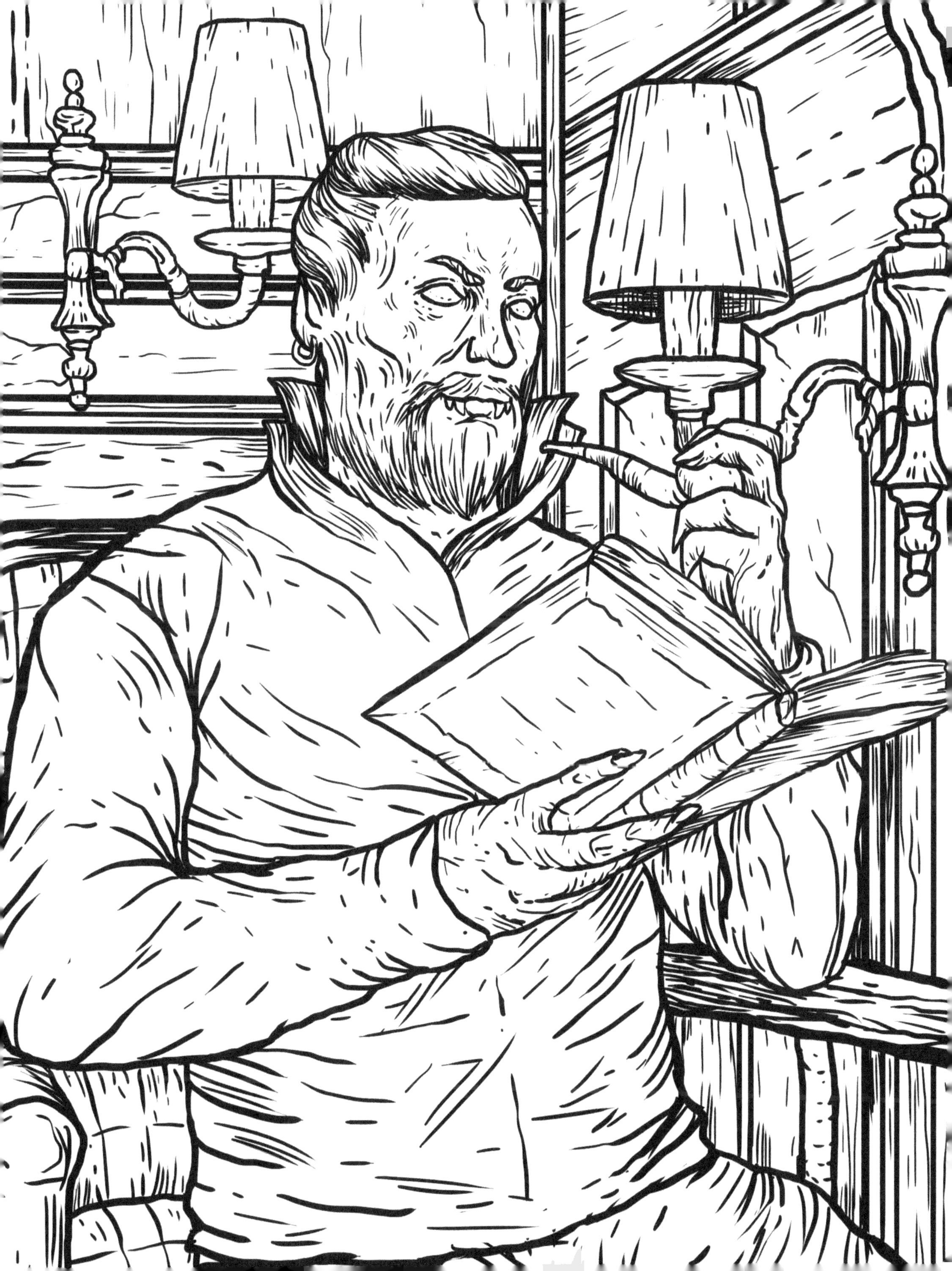

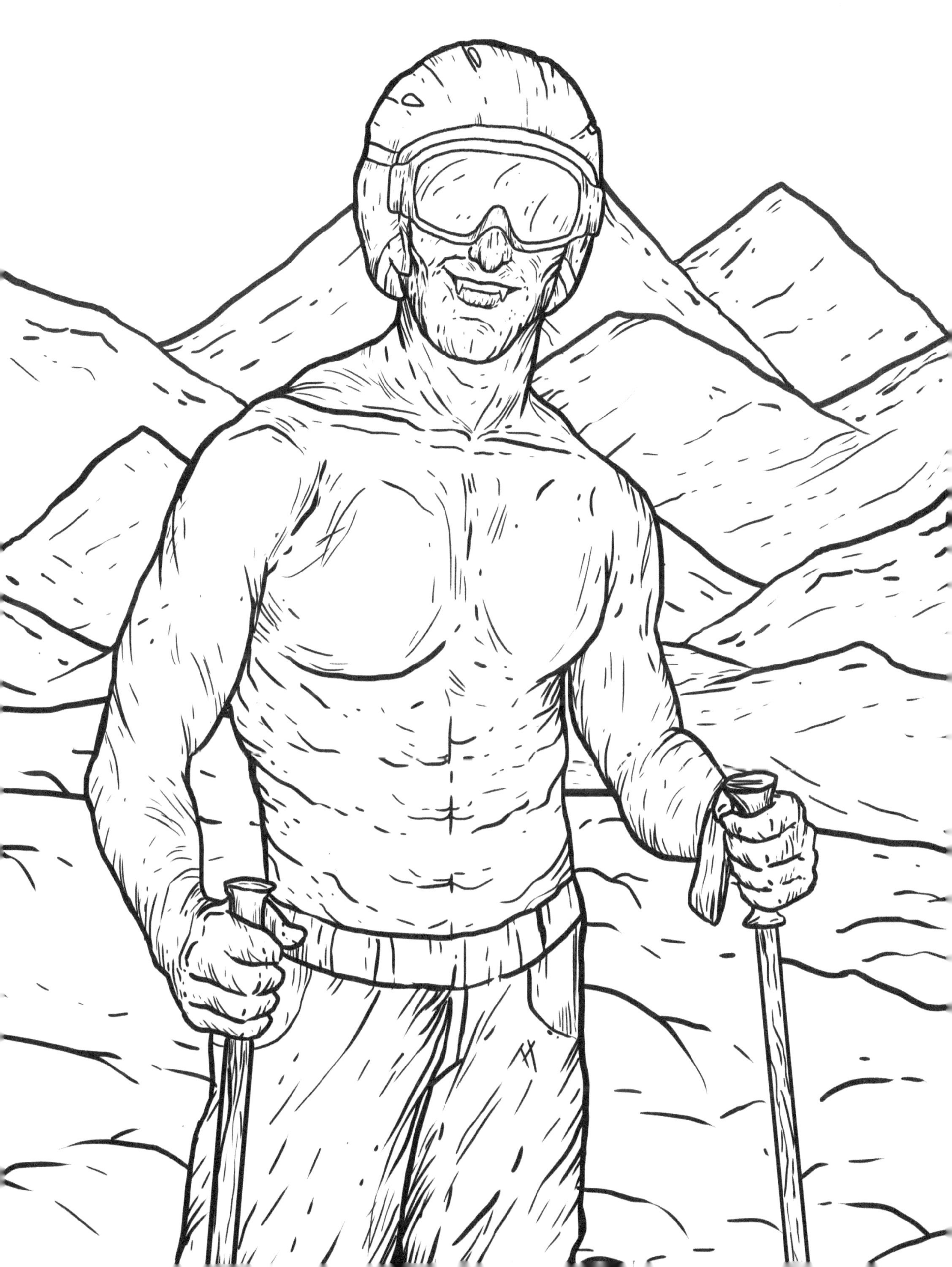

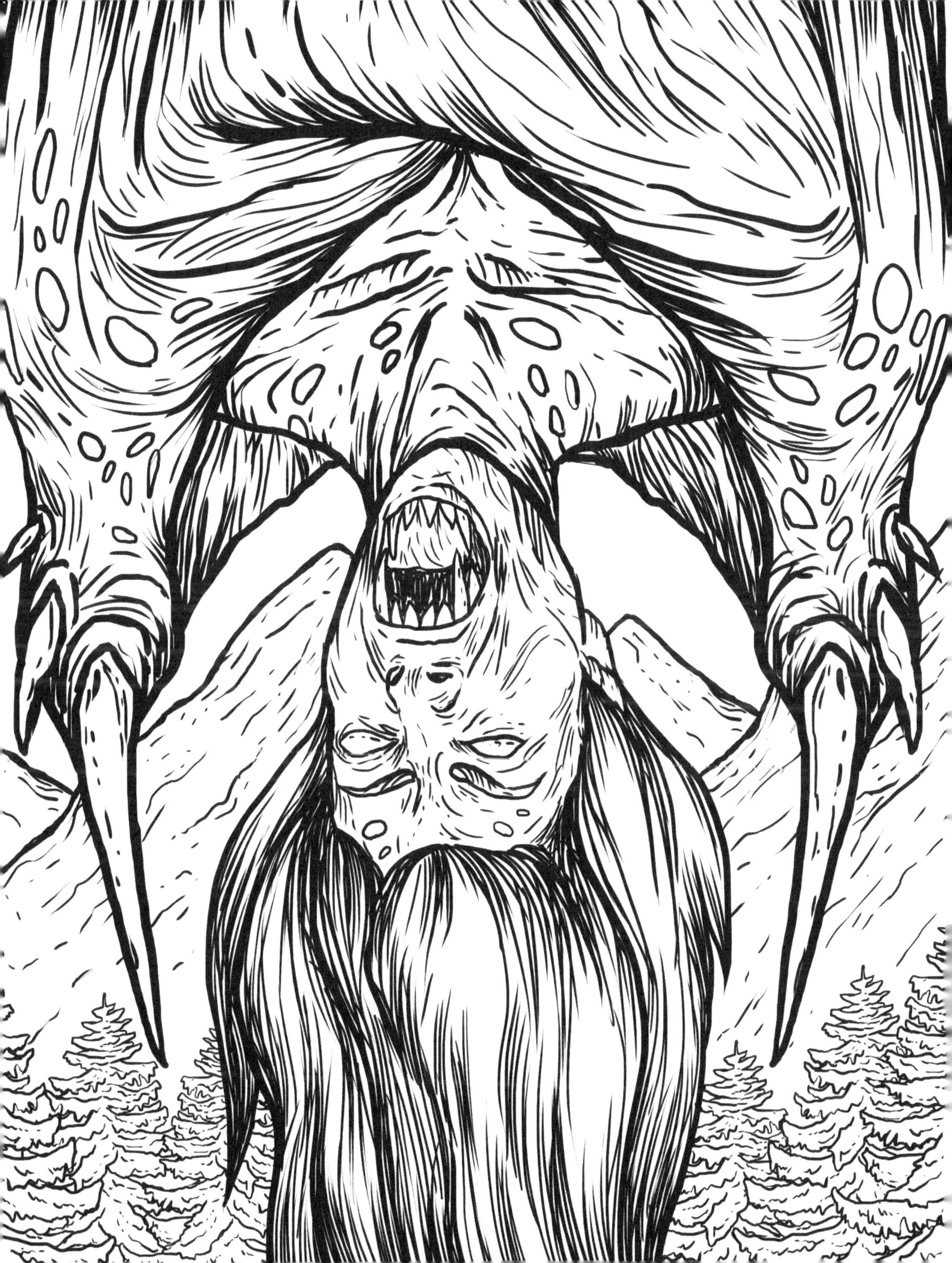